Fadó

My Irish Once upon a Time

Scarlet Rosalie Biedron

iUniverse books may be ordered through booksellers or by contacting:

iUniverse
1663 Liberty Drive
Bloomington, IN 47403
www.iuniverse.com
1-800-Authors (1-800-288-4677)

Because of the dynamic nature of the Internet, any web addresses or links contained in this book may have changed since publication and may no longer be valid. The views expressed in this work are solely those of the author and do not necessarily reflect the views of the publisher, and the publisher hereby disclaims any responsibility for them.

Any people depicted in stock imagery provided by Getty Images are models, and such images are being used for illustrative purposes only.
Certain stock imagery © Getty Images.

ISBN: 978-1-5320-6257-5 (sc)
978-1-5320-6258-2 (e)

Library of Congress Control Number: 2018915101

Print information available on the last page.

iUniverse rev. date: 12/27/2018

Dedication Page

I wrote this book to share some of the meaningful lessons I have learned throughout the early years of my riding career. I hope that it inspires others to reflect on their own lives and personal life lessons and that they put down the book having gained some new perspective or insight. This book is dedicated to my parents, family, friends, and mentors, without whom the formation of this book could not have been made possible. Thank you.

Table of Contents

Follow Your Passion: Why I Began Riding

I didn't start show jumping because I fell in love with it the first time I ever rode a horse or jumped a fence. Nor did I start because I was naturally good at it. I didn't become a show jumper for any reason derived from a fairytale or a fantacy. At first, I didn't even like jumping. I did, however, like horses. I loved horses. I was also extremely competitive. When my love for horses and my competitiveness collided, I became a show jumper. From that moment onward, I loved it. I more than loved it, I was enthralled by it, and there was no going back.

It began when I was extremely young. My mother liked to say that as soon as we could walk we could get up on a horse, and she would take me to our family farm to take a trail ride or to have lessons on our pony, Beau. When I was ten years old I went fox hunting for the first time. Galloping across the fields and through the forest, the love and thrill of riding ignited inside me. While I wanted to be able to jump, I secretly did not enjoy jumping. It scared the living daylights out of me. On the fox hunting field, I used to pray we would not come across another log because I didn't want to have to jump it.

When I got a bit older, I started spending more time at our family farm. I would go there after school and all day in the summers. I loved the horses and being around them. I had a pony named Peaches, and I wanted to spend all day, every day, with her. I would occasionally take her to a local show with my trainer, Ann, but I much preferred just taking lessons at home, riding her at the farm, and fox hunting. I remembered one show in particular: Peaches and I came out of a cross rail class. Ann was telling me about my round. She said that it was really good but to remember that we had discussed cutting the corners and being efficient. She was trying to get me to be competitive at the show. I could not have cared less about that. I was hungry for the speed and the feeling of freedom I experienced while Peaches and I were flying around our farm.

The Winter Equestrian Festival (WEF) in Wellington, Florida, is an important series of shows in the world of competitive show jumping, not only in the US, but internationally as well. At the time I had never heard of any shows outside of the few local New Jersey shows at which I had competed. I still, to this day, remember Ann and our stable manager, Chris, talking to me about it for the first time. We were in the indoor ring. Chris and Ann walked next to me as we were walking out of the indoor toward the barn. I was riding Peaches.

"So, Rose," Chris said, "What do you think about doing a show?"

Ann looked nervous. I just smiled and nodded silently, because Chris, like jumping, scared the living daylights out of me. She turned her head away from me as she continued talk, and we were walking, so I couldn't really hear all of what she was saying. I did catch the tail end of it, "It's in Wellington. You know WEF." She paused, "Do you know WEF?"

I had no clue what she was talking about.

"Sorry, what's a WEF?" I asked.

She burst out laughing and looked at Ann. Her laugh was extremely distinctive. I can still recall the way her laugh sounds. She explained, "WEF stands for the Winter Equestrian Festival. It a big show in Florida. It will be fun. Ann and I spoke to your mom about it because you will already be in Florida for Spring Break." She looked right at me, "Okay?"

"Okay," I said.

I had no clue what I was getting into. When we went to WEF for the first time I was twelve years old and in the sixth grade. My mother agreed that I could go for the two weeks of Spring Break, but there was still one final week of WEF after that. Chris and Ann thought I should be allowed to stay for the extra week. My mother agreed that if I did well during the first two weeks of competing I could stay for the final week. I showed Peaches in the .80 meter class. The first day I showed her, I won the class. I couldn't believe it. WEF is one of the biggest shows in the US. .80 meters was big for me at the time.

I won the next day as well. With that win came a feeling of pressure. If I did well the following day I would be Champion for the week. I asked my mother that night, "What if I mess up? What if I make a mistake, or fall off?" She said that this was all just for fun and to remember that I was doing this because I loved riding Peaches. She said, "As soon as this isn't fun anymore, choose a different game." Just as my love of riding was sparked on the fox hunting field, my passion for show jumping had been ignited in Wellington. I have loved show jumping ever since. If you do what you love, you will always love what you do.

Always Get Back In the Saddle

In 2016, I competed at WEF with six different horses. I learned many lessons in those 12 weeks. One of the most valuable lessons I learned was to always get back in the saddle, to metaphorically get back in the saddle, that is. In reality, there are times to push through and get back on, and there are times to rethink the plan and go back to the drawing board. One challenge I faced in my riding was maintaining a concrete and confident attitude even after a fall.

One day, mid-circuit at WEF, I stood motionless in the in-gate, attempting to set aside my nerves. I was moments away from walking into the ring, and, despite being extensively prepared, I was mentally plagued by doubt. I was on the precipice of giving up and walking away; in my heart, I truly wanted to do just that. I could hear my horse's heart racing underneath me. Eager to get in the show ring, my horse, Buttercup, chomped at the bit. My uncertainty and fear of failure placed my feelings and attitude in direct contrast with those of my horse; I was anything but chomping at the bit to get into the ring and jump around the daunting course yet again. I struggled to concentrate while being overwhelmed by the flashing memories and the fear and upset of what had just happened. I tried to focus on the present moment. It wasn't working.

I had begun that very same day with an early morning course walk. I got on my first horse, Quinton, with excitement. As I warmed up, my confidence grew in anticipation of the competition. I galloped into the ring with a fearless attitude. The beginning of my course was good, but I landed short after fence four. Having misjudged the next distance, I didn't cover enough ground to get the seven strides to fence five. I was too far away from the fence. My horse attempted to compensate by over jumping, and I got knocked loose from the saddle. Flying through the air became surreal, the fall seeming to unfold in slow motion as I braced for the impact with the ground. Rudely awoken from my dream-like state by the strike of reality, the entire weight of my horse came crushing down as his hoof landed on my hand. Sand covering me, embedded in my jacket and helmet, I walked out of the ring clutching my hand close to my body.

"Are you okay?" my trainer asked. The rhetorical question brought me face to face with her concerned and disappointed expression.

"Yeah..." I cleared my throat and with it the self-doubt in my voice, "Yes." But I was still guarding my hand holding it close to my body, which she didn't miss.

"Can you move it?" I brought my hand up in front of me, spreading my fingers wide, and quickly tucked it away again.

"Great. Get back on," she said.

I remounted and jumped a few fences in the warm-up arena to make sure Quinton was unfazed by my unexpected fall. The numb aftershock which had kept my tears at bay, wore off as I got on my second horse, Buttercup. As I warmed up, I fought back this overload of emotions. The stabbing pain in my hand did not compare to the pain of my own disappointment. Rattled and embarrassed, I could not help but replay the scenario over and over in my head. I battled to recompose myself and focus on fixing my mistake in my next round.

I mentally reviewed the course one last time as stood in the in-gate waiting to enter the arena. I was unsure of myself and my ability to overcome the looming consequence of my fall. I walked into the show arena. When the buzzer sounded, I began my course for the second time. Holding my breath, I cantered to the first fence. The beginning of my course unfolded similarly to my first attempt. As I turned the corner to fence four, my innate determination took hold, and there was not a hesitant bone in my body. I had a strong jump into the bending line and locked in on the seven strides early to meet fence five with a perfect distance. Relief washed over me as I landed on the far side of the fence- still firmly in my saddle. Having rectified my mistake, I navigated the course with my regained confidence. Putting in, what I later learned to be, the winning ride, I came out of the ring having survived. On the edge of surrender and on the brink of giving up after my fall, I survived. The action I describe as surviving, I now look back on as perseverance.

Just before I entered the ring with Buttercup, I was overwhelmed by self-doubt, over-thinking, and fear. I continued onward, not because I knew I could, not because I believed in myself, and certainly, not for any lack of fear of failure or disappointment. I endured because I was unquestionably more afraid of the alternative. I was afraid of giving up. I was more afraid of giving up than I was of falling off. So, I didn't give up. It is ironic that fear usual leads people to quit: fear of failure, fear of disappointment, fear of injury, or another unknown fear. However, it was fear that aided me in continuing on.

In a situation where I want to give up or get off of the horse and quit, even though I am afraid of failure or of disappointment, or even of getting hurt, I am more afraid of giving up. I find the courage to continue in the face of fear because I would rather fail over and over again, than to give up even once. When failure or a fall has made me doubt myself, I get back in the saddle because I am more afraid of giving up than anything else. The ability to get back on despite self-doubt is one of the most important and valuable lessons riding has taught me thus far.

3

The Move To Ireland: Feeling American

The decision to move to Europe was not difficult. I had gone to Ireland several times to look at show jumping horses and to do some training with a top professional, and future Olympian, Greg Broderick. In the summer of 2016, I made the plan with my parents and a few other critical people, including Greg, to move my riding program and show jumping career to Europe. The plan was to be doing a lot of back and forth between living in Ireland, traveling to compete in Europe, and returning to spend time at home in New Jersey. I had every intention of going back home to New Jersey for one week every month, but it didn't turn out that way.

On September 7, 2016, I took a flight from Newark Liberty Airport to Dublin International Airport, marking the first step in a life-changing journey. I walked out of the Dublin airport with a feeling of endless possibility and freedom. I was accompanied by a young woman who had managed my horses and show jumping program in the United States, Annette Fusco. I am not exactly sure if she had a feeling of endless possibility or one of serious concern. Regardless, neither of us had any idea what was in store for us. We did not visit home for several months, and I had my first Christmas away from home and apart from my family. It felt strange to have uprooted myself so suddenly and changed my life so completely.

For the first several months Annette and I lived in The Horse and Jockey, a wonderful Irish hotel, complete with a bakery-café, a quaint gift shop, a pub bustling with local color, and an ever-present, grandfatherly proprietor. On a normal day we went to the barn where I trained, riding the horses in the mornings and doing school work in the afternoons. I was settling into a routine that, along with the green rolling hills of the surrounding countryside, felt familiar and comfortable. We had dinner either at the hotel, just fifteen minutes from the small town of Thurles, or at one of the two restaurants in town. While many things in Ireland seemed similar to the United States, it was also very different. The weather was always overcast, and I do mean always! It was challenging to get acclimated to the drastically shorter days as we moved through fall and into winter, and to the gloomy, dark, and dreary overtone of the weather.

Although English was the primary language in Ireland, there was a serious language barrier. The sense humor, language use, and cultural phrases and sayings were extremely different. I learned new definitions and nuances of words that do not carry the same meanings as they do in America. In Ireland, "grand" means *okay* or *just fine but not great*. "What's the crack?" means *what's the drama, gossip,* or *news*? "Lads" means *guys*; "no bother," *no problem*. And the best word in all of Ireland is, "Well." The word, "Well," tantamount to any greeting, response, question, joke, or answer an Irish person ever needs, is a complete, stand-alone sentence. "Well" became my secret weapon. I was able to say *Good morning, Thank you, I'm fine,* and *See you later* by just saying, "Well."

The accents of the Irish people, particularly in the area in which we live, are extremely strong. It was very challenging to adjust to talking with people whom I could barely understand. It was difficult at times, to accept the looks I got when someone realized I was an American. As a result, I got to work on my Irish accent right away. I became so skilled at an Irish accent that Irish people who would meet me for the first time wouldn't believe that I was actually American. They were convinced that I was from Tipperary, or maybe Kilkenny, possibly Cork: anywhere in Ireland, but definitely not from America. Having an American accent had made me feel isolated and separate from the people who and the culture that surrounded me. By developing an excellent Irish accent, I was able to feel more accepted, at home, and integrated into the culture.

Although it was wonderful to have that feeling of being accepted and of belonging, moving to Ireland was a complete culture shock, and it was an experience that made me feel like I was truly an American. The most comforting feature of moving to Ireland was that Annette moved over with me. Two other young women from California, Veronica and Adrienne, had also recently moved over. There was an instant bond among the four of us; being Americans living abroad really brought us close together immediately. Suddenly, having an American accent was a 'thing'. Suddenly, when I competed in shows, I was not just *"Rosalie Biedron"* over the loud speaker. I was *"Rosalie Biedron, for the United States of America!"* Never in my entire 16 years of life, had I ever felt more American than when I moved away from America. The experience of moving to Ireland and immersing myself in cultures throughout Europe for months at a time made me feel as though I was from a home, a place, and a country. It took me leaving the United States to gain this perspective. America is now a much bigger and a more important part of my identity, in my own eyes and perhaps in the eyes of others.

4

Being Part of a Team

When we would drive around Ireland, anyone we passed on back roads would wave and smile. Often, Annette and I would look at each other and ask, *"Do we know them?"* It took us a while to realize that people were simply friendly. Acclimating to the very different cultural climate of County Tipperary we quickly realized that all you have to say by way of greeting is, "Well." Everywhere else, "How ye going?" works just fine in almost any circumstance. These two expressions cover an enormous amount of conversational ground, without relying on the formality of memorizing or using names, or worrying about whether or not you had met the person previously.

After I had lived in Ireland for some time, the culture shock faded. Truth be told, it nearly disappeared. I began to feel as though I was a part of the Irish group. I met and was introduced to so many new people, I couldn't even begin to keep their names straight in my head. Regardless, the other American girls and I became a part of Ireland, and Ireland became a part of us. There is a true closeness, a comraderie among all Irish people, and I feel that the four of us were able to experience this closeness very quickly as well. Once we became, what felt like, honorary Irish, it was a whole new level of closeness. In the States most people go to a horse show to see their horse, child or friend compete. They arrived just before the class began, and they'd leave after it was over. In Ireland everybody showed up for the whole day. When one Irish person won, every Irish person won. So, suddenly it wasn't just my family and friends cheering me on, it was pretty much every Irish person in the show jumping world. It was a truly amazing thing to experience.

Looking back on the close-knit group of people in the show jumping world of which we became a part, it seems normal. However, at the time, it was exciting, new, amazing, and very much fun. For any Irish person, the closeness of all Irish people seems normal. However, we had moved over from America. Moreover, I was from the East Coast. In New York City you don't make eye contact with strangers and you certainly don't smile and wave. If you bumped shoulders with someone walking down the street, and it caused you to drop your books or your bag, they would might look at you and yell. And that's if they are being nice. Then, every single person on the crowded street who is walking by would simply walk around you or maybe even over you. Ireland could not have been a bigger contrast. If you were in the same scenario in Dublin, the person with whom you bumped shoulders would likely apologize and ask if you are alright. Then they might help you pick up anything you dropped.

One particular day in Vejer, Spain, at the Sunshine Tour in 2017, my mother, Annette, Veronica, Molly, Adrienne, Greg, and I were all sitting at a table having lunch. Some of us had just started lunch and others had finished. It was a casual lunch, and were all together because we all rode at the same barn. This was a concept that had become familiar: eat and spend time with the people from the same barn. By the time I was finishing my lunch, more people we knew started to sit down. They all happened to be Irish. Then, a few more Irish friends pulled up chairs. Within minutes, I was meeting more Irish people for the first time than I could count.

However, it wasn't an American meet and greet where you introduce yourself, quickly make small talk, and then politely pretend you have somewhere else to be. Lunch had taken on what I came to think of as that typical Irish flow: people coming in when they could, eating when they were hungry, and then settling in. Once I got a person's name it was as though I had known them for years. There was laughing, joking, teasing, stories, funny videos being passed around on peoples' phones.

I didn't think much of it at the time. But, looking back it struck me how very different it was. I truly felt a part of the group. During my time in Ireland, I became a part of this cohesive culture. I became a part of the team. It did not disconnect me from my feelings of being American or of being a part of my family. It didn't make me feel feel less connected with my friends in America. It was the addition of a new team, and it added to the fullness of my entire life. It helped me see that there was another way to be and to interact in the world. If anything, it made me feel more connected everywhere.

5

Learn From Your Mistakes

Making mistakes is a part of the learning process. It is just as important to learn from your success, as it is to learn from your failures and mistakes. Often, as a competitor, you have more difficult days in which you make mistakes than perfect days. In fact, the days where your performance is perfect are rare if they ever exist at all. In show jumping, I make mistakes at home training and in the ring. Although it feels frustrating to make mistakes, it is an important part of the learning process.

One day, I was having a lesson with Greg on my horse Frenchie. We were in the indoor, and the lesson was going very well. We were doing a final course as part of the lesson. The last jump in the course was a tight turn back to a tall vertical. I came around the tight turn with one stride and jumped the fence. Frenchie over jumped it and started bucking on the back side. Greg called me into the center of the ring. He explained that he wanted me to turn the corner with Frenchie bent around my inside leg, get straight, and just pop over the vertical so that on the back side of the fence I landed in control.

I thought I was near the end of my lesson, that I would repeat the turn once, get it right, and I would be finished. I was very, very wrong. I did the turn again, but Frenchie was quick and fresh and landed shaking his head and not in control.

Greg called out loudly, "Rose, you need to slow it all down, come around the corner, get straight, just pop the vertical, and land with the horse listening. Again."

So, I repeated the turn and jumped the vertical, but still did not get it right. Greg said, "He is not listening to you at all! It is not that it is bad or you are missing the distance or anything, but it is important that you get this just right."

I did that turn over and over, but it still wasn't right. It wasn't soft and smooth. It was rushed. Still, on the landing side, Frenchie wasn't listening. So, Greg had me work him on the flat, get him listening to my leg, lengthening and shortening his stride. Insisting that he listen. After twenty minutes, I was dripping in sweat, my face was bright right, and I was out of breath. Finally, Frenchie was listening.

We tried the turn again. This time, I turned the corner with Frenchie bent around my inside leg, I got straight, and just popped over the vertical. Then, when we landed he was balanced, quiet, and in control. It was all smooth and I had done it right.

Greg called me over to the center of the ring and said, "I want you to remember that feeling. That is what it should feel like every time in the show ring and at home. Now, do it one more time just to make sure it wasn't luck." I did the turn again, and it was perfect.

In that lesson, I made the same mistake sixteen times. It was frustrating and exhausting, but extremely valuable for improving my riding ability. It was critically important in my relationship with my horse. Imagine if the first time I did that turn, I had gotten it right? Then, I would have never had the experience of working through it with my horse and learning how to get it right when it wasn't perfect the first time. If I hadn't made those mistakes, I wouldn't have the confidence to work through problems with Frenchie when I needed to. Humans are experiential learners. If we never made mistakes, we would not gain the valuable experience of correcting and working through our mistakes. We would never have the confidence to overcome problems if we never face adversity. Making mistakes is a large and important part of how we learn.

6

Practice Mentality vs. Competition Mentality

I used to have the same mentality for training and practice as I did for a competition: I am never good enough. There is always something I can improve. This may be true, but is it the best competition mentality? No. I recently read a sports psychology book, *How Champions Think: In Sports and in Life* by Dr. Bob Rotella. In his book, Dr. Rotella suggests that the best mentality for competition and game day is confidence and believing that your abilities are good enough that you can win. I thought that this was an interesting idea that definitely applies to show jumping. For example, if my horse has a massive stride, but isn't great at tight turns, I will utilize their strengths and leave out strides in the jump off. Or if my horse is quick with a small stride, I will execute very tight turns, but might not leave out the strides.

Whatever the case, in competition, you must utilize your strengths to get the job done and win. If you aren't perfect at a jump or have to change your plan, you don't throw your hands up and quit in the middle of a round. You do your best anyway.

Before going into the show ring to compete, show jumpers warm up in a practice ring and jump a few practice fences. I normally get on the horse somewhere between thirty and forty minutes before I have to go in the ring so I can warm up. In this time period, I am probably not going to learn anything new that will drastically improve my riding. So, there is no point in having the mentality that I am not good enough and need to improve. Instead, a confident mindset will help me.

One day, at a competition in Barnadown, Ireland, I decided to take on this competition mentality. I was warming my horses up to go into the show ring. Whenever I doubted myself or thought of the ways I wasn't perfect, I thought to myself, 'I may not be perfect, I may make mistakes, I am definitely not the best rider in the world, and there are definitely ways I can improve, but I am good enough to jump around this course, get it done, and win.' This competition mentality of confidence and believing that I am good enough to do the task at hand really helped me focus and have confidence that day.

As a competitor, I believe that having a good mentality and a confident outlook is very important. Yet there is a drastic difference between my mentality in practice, when I am training, and the mentality I have when going into a competition. In practice and in training, I take on the attitude of always striving to improve: I am never good enough. Practice is the time to set yourself up for success by learning and improving. However, when it comes to going in the show ring, it is important to be confident and believe in yourself. In those thirty minutes of warming up, there is no better way to set yourself up for success than to focus on the task at hand. Now, I always go in the show ring with the belief that my skills and abilities- although not perfect- are good enough for me to win and get the job done.

7

The Power Of Meaningful Conversations

I was having dinner with Veronica and Greg at a hotel in Northern Ireland, where we were staying for a horse show. Alice, Greg's girlfriend, was meeting us later. Greg, Veronica, and I sat at a table in a corner and all ordered the Caesar salad, which we had heard was really good. Sitting at the table we chatted for a while, and when our Caesar salads came we ate in silence for a few minutes.

Out of nowhere, Greg asked a rather thought-provoking the question:

"If you could be a different person for one day who would it be?"

I am not sure if Veronica was as surprised by this question as I was, but she repeated it back, "If I could be a different person for one day, who would it be?"

"Yeah," Greg said.

"Do they have to be alive?" I asked.

Greg thought for a minute, "No, they don't have to be alive."

It was an impressively thought-provoking question. "So, Veronica?" Greg said.

"Amal Clooney," she said.

Greg and I both probably had an equality clueless looks on our faces, because Veronica went on to explain, "Amal Clooney is George Clooney's wife. She is so beautiful, and cool, and smart, and she has an amazing and influential job."

"Ah, very cool," I said.

"Alright, Rosie?" Greg looked at me raised his eyebrows.

"I guess I would pick Isaac Newton or Winston Churchill," I said.

"Why's that?" Greg asked.

"One was an influential leader in history who helped shape the world; and he was a powerful speaker. The other was a brilliant scientist and physicist who helped shape the world. Both had brilliant minds, and I would like to know what it is like to think like them."

"Very good," Greg said.

"Ok, let's hear it Greggers," Veronica said, "We know you've got your answer ready to go."

"I'm not exactly sure *who* it would be, but I'd either like to be someone very old or very young. I would want to be able to gain the perspective of someone much older than myself looking back on life and know the things they know," Greg said.

I thought both Veronica and Greg had very good and wise answers.

While I was away from the table, Alice arrived and was asked the same question. When I returned to the table, Veronica said, "Rose, you will never believe which person Alice picked."

"Who?" I asked as I tried to think who she might have picked.

"Greg?" I guessed. Everyone laughed at my guess.

"No, Amal Clooney. The same person I choose," Veronica said.

"Are you serious?" I asked. I found it hard to believe that Veronica and Alice both picked the same person.

"No really, I did!," Alice said.

"It's funny how Alice and I chose someone for who they are and what they do for the world; Rose chose someone for their brain; and Greg chose someone to gain a new perspective on life," Veronica said.

I thought it was interesting to ask people thought provoking questions, but it takes just the right circumstances, with the right group of people, at the right time to spark a truly meaningful, and in-depth conversation. We did not stay on the topic much longer, and it might not have led any of us to discuss the universe or to understand the meaning of life any better, but it did lead us to think about our lives, our place in the world, and to contemplate new perspectives.

Several weeks later, Veronica brought up the conversation again and said how interesting she thought it was. If she hadn't of brought it up again I might have taken it for granted. When thinking back to that horse show, it would have been washed out of my mind. Instead, I look back, and it makes me think about what it would be like to be 30, 50, 70, or even 100 years old and looking back on my own life. What advice would I give to myself? What would I do differently? What moments would I burn into my memory? I always try and hold onto and think back to meaningful conversations that I have had. Even if they seem small or insignificant, they cause me to stop and think about who I am, about my place in the world, and about who I want to be. This ability to take a moment, slow down, and appreciate the small moments in life is invaluable.

8

Facing My Own Self-Imposed Limitations

In June, Annette and I drove from Ireland to Belgium, where I would compete at a horse show called Knokke for three weeks. Veronica and Adrienne were also making the drive; so, we all took the same ferry from Dublin to England in our separate cars. In England, Adrienne went to spend the night at her boyfriend, Spencer's, house. Veronica went to stay the night at a hotel near the Eurotunnel. Annette and I drove to Oxford.

We checked into the hotel and settled into the room with my dog, Ginger. Immediately, Annette gave me a detailed itinerary of our short day in the small, lovely English city. It included sites to see, places to eat, cultural stops, and a visit to Oxford University. The next day we set off exploring. We went to the museum across the street from our hotel and then to a restaurant called Lighthouse. We sat at a table overlooking the river. The sun beat down, and it was extremely hot, but worth it. We walked around the city toward some of the University sites. On our way, we walked down an extremely touristy street lined with shops that sold all kinds of gear and tickets branded with the University logo. I bought an Oxford University oversized t-shirt and workout shorts. Such a touristy endeavor was rather out of character, but necessary as I had forgotten to put pajamas in my smaller overnight bag. We had a great day in this spontaneous way, seeing so many beautiful buildings, take pictures, laughing.

Sitting back in our hotel room, I thought about our brief trip to Oxford. It didn't take years of planning or cause us any excessive amounts of stress. In fact, it wasn't stressful at all. In order to plan a fun trip like this, all you had to do was figure out what you wanted to do and do it. It was a simple concept with regard to how people wish to live their lives, but it was an important one. Figure out what it is that you enjoy doing, what you love, what you're passionate about, or what makes you happy, and do it.

The next day, we woke up very early and drove toward the Eurotunnel. We arrived there with a car full of suitcases, two people, and one dog. We followed the signs. Once aboard the train, the attendants came and told us to turn the car off. Then they closed the dividers between every three cars. After what seemed like a short time, the train jolted and began to move. My ears popped several times.

"I think we are going below sea level," I said

"Yeah, I think you might be right," Annette responded.

In reality, the train ride was over and we were in France. What I thought would be a scary new experience was actually pretty simple. On a later train, Veronica followed. Adriene drove over as well. By the end of that day, we were all in Knokke searching for parking. Each of us had taken on a new experience. It was a seemly insignificant experience, and looking back it's easy to brush aside. Yet, at the time, we drove into the unknown. It could have been stressful or scary, but it wasn't. This seemed to me the perfect metaphor for what each had accomplished. All three of these young women who I admired had left their comfort zone, the known, moved away from family friends, and home, and made a life in a foreign country, traveling across Europe and to unknown places and new experiences fairly easily. They were fiercely independent, as I am, and they made the most of each new experience. They knew how to be their own advocates and how to problem solve. They knew how to live their own lives.

When I was really young and traveling with my family, I would get stressed out in airports. The confusion about where to go, what to do, how to get there were all very overwhelming. I once asked my mother, "How will I ever be able to be an adult?" She asked what I meant. I said, "Well, how will I be able to go through airports on my own?"

"Ah…" she said, "You know, airports are designed for absolutely everyone to navigate and find their destination. You will have no problem doing that." I knew she was right, because these are simply things moms know. From then on, I felt confident going through airports. As I grew older, I still wondered how I would possibly be an adult and live my life. There were so many aspects of being an adult which seemed so foreign to me. By traveling across Europe with Annette, Veronica, Adrienne, and our three dogs, I learned one of the most important life lessons: I am fully capable of living my own life. It was only my self-imposed limitation, my fear, that was holding me back, keeping me from feeling that confidence. There was no physical event which shifted my perspective, but it wasn't until I sat in the passenger seat driving from Ireland to Belgium through the Eurotunnel that I realized there was nothing holding me back from taking on new experiences and living life with confidence, confidence in myself and in my abilities. Life is designed to be navigated by *absolutely everyone*, just like the airport. I feel confident in my ability to navigate my own life.

9

Success

Success looks different to every person. For me, success is riding a course of jumps in the show ring exactly according to plan, win or lose. Success is following my passion. It is being a good friend, daughter, sister, or cousin. It is standing by my own integrity no matter the circumstances. It is working hard. It is making the same mistake over and over and still not giving up. To be successful, is to have an unquenchable thirst to learn, to be better than you were yesterday.

In the second week competing at Knokke in Belgium, I won the CSI 1* Grand Prix on my horse, Wizard. I also won another class on him early that week, and placed 3[d] and 6th on my horse, Charmeur, in CSI 2* classes. However, I made several mistakes that week on my horse, Tucson Z. I made simple mistakes that I shouldn't have made. Was it a successful week? Despite winning, I had made many mistakes. Did winning outweigh my mistakes? These were questions I asked myself at the end of the week. I came to the conclusion that winning did not determine my success that week at Knokke. What did determine my success was whether or not I had learned from my mistakes. If I became a better rider for having made those mistakes, then it was truly a successful week.

When I step back and think about the lessons I have learned through riding, moving to Ireland, and competing in Europe, I only feel gratitude. I would not be who I am without the support of so many people like my family, my close friends, my mentors, my trainers, and my horses. I certainly would not have grown to be the person I am, without being afforded so many opportunities to succeed. Most of these opportunities have been as a student. They have allowed me to learn as an academic student and a riding student. I measure my own success by my ability to improve, to grow, and to learn. To be successful, is to be continual and humble student.

Scarlet Rosalie Biedron currently lives in Ireland where she trains as a competitive show jumper. She was born and raised in Oldwick, New Jersey. She has a love for art, literature, and writing. When she is not riding a horse or doing school work, you can find her painting and pondering her place in the world.

Printed in the United States
By Bookmasters